Salt Marsh Trends in Selected Estuaries of Southwestern Connecticut

Ralph W. Tiner
U.S. Fish and Wildlife Service
National Wetlands Inventory Program
300 Westgate Center Drive
Hadley, MA 01035

Irene J. Huber, Todd Nuerminger, and Eric Marshall
Department of Plant and Soil Sciences
Stockbridge Hall
University of Massachusetts
Amherst, MA 01003

April 2006

National Wetlands Inventory Cooperative Report

Prepared for the Long Island Studies Program, Connecticut Department of Environmental Protection, Hartford, CT

TABLE OF CONTENTS

LIST OF FIGURES

LIST OF TABLES

INTRODUCTION

Recent investigations have shown that rising sea levels are having a significant impact on tidal wetlands in many areas of the United States. Higher water levels are inundating lower portions of these marshes and converting them to tidal flats, while portions of the high marsh are being converted to low marsh. The importance of coastal marshes to marine and estuarine ecosystems and migratory waterfowl is widely recognized. Because of these and other values (e.g., storm surge detention), most coastal states have adopted specific legislation to protect these highly valued natural resources. The State of Connecticut was among the first states to pass such legislation and has been protecting its tidal wetlands since 1970. While this law has virtually eliminated the once-widespread dredging and filling of tidal wetlands, nature's forces (i.e., rising sea level) continues to impact these wetlands.

The Long Island Studies (LIS) Program of the Connecticut Department of Environmental Protection (DEP) has noticed the habitat changes indicative of sea-level rise in many coastal wetlands. In 2005, DEP provided funds to the U.S. Fish and Wildlife Service to conduct a trends analysis of selected salt marshes along the southwestern coast of the state to document habitat changes. The Natural Resources Assessment Group (NRAG) at University of Massachusetts provides technical support to the U.S. Fish and Wildlife Service's National Wetlands Inventory (NWI) Program and assisted with this trends analysis project.

Study Objectives

To document changes in marsh vegetation zones (low marsh and high marsh) in six salt marsh areas in southwestern Connecticut since 1974. The following time periods would be evaluated: 1) 1974-1981, 2) 1981-1986, 3) 1986-1990, 4) 1990-1995, 5) 1995-2000, and 6) 2000-2004. Photointerpretation of vegetation changes would document the total changes between intervals and over the past quarter century as well as identify any differences in the rate of change during the entire study period.

Study Areas

The six study areas were located along the western shore of Long Island Sound in southwestern Connecticut (Figure 1): 1) Cos Cob Harbor (Greenwich; 126-acre intertidal area), 2) Grays Creek (Westport; 35-acre intertidal zone), 3) Scott Cove (Darien; 121-acre intertidal area), 4) Five Mile River (Darien/Norwalk; 18-acre intertidal zone), 5) Greenwich Cove (100-acre intertidal area), and 6) Canfield Island Cove (Norwalk; 109-acre intertidal area). The spring tide range in this area is about 8.0 feet (i.e., 8.3 feet in Cos Cob Harbor; http://co-ops.nos.noaa.gov/tide_pred.html), which is more than twice the range as in Long Island Sound estuaries east of the Connecticut River. The mean tide range is approximately 7.0 feet (i.e., 7.2 feet for Cos Cob Harbor).

Figure 1. General location of study estuaries along the Connecticut coast (see Appendix A for detailed maps).

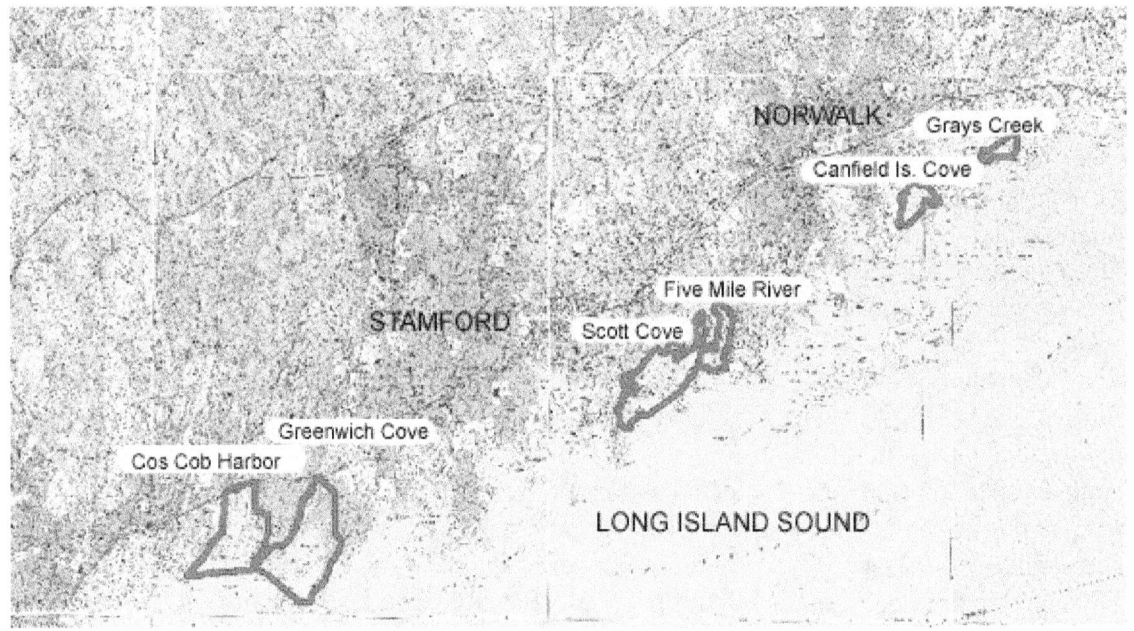

METHODS

Digital images of aerial photography for the study areas were provided by the LIS Program for the following years: 1974, 1981, 1986, 1990, 1995, 2000, and 2004. These images were georeferenced in Connecticut State Plane Coordinates (NAD 83). The boundaries of salt marsh complexes for each of the sites were delineated and saved as a shapefile in Connecticut State Plane Coordinates (NAD 83) for each of the study sites and for each year of photography.

For each study site, aerial photographs were interpreted on-screen and the following features were delineated for each era: low marsh, high marsh, and tidal flat. The area of each feature was then calculated for each study area and for each time period. In most cases, the aerial photographs were captured at low tide, so the limits of tidal flats could be detected. In eras where the aerial photos were not low-tide synchronized, the tidal flats from the other time periods were assumed to be present. Where human-induced changes were detected, the extent and nature of the change was recorded.

A geospatial data base was created to store data on wetland changes. This data base was used to generate maps and statistics of salt marsh trends. Statistics were generated to reflect the area of low marsh, area of high marsh, area of tidal flat (depending on stage of tide), the overall area of tidal wetland for each time period, and the extent of human-induced changes. These data were then used to demonstrate wetland changes between years (at approximately five-year intervals). A series of maps showing the changes for each salt marsh complex was generated. A metadata file for this project was also created to document source data and other pertinent information about the project and interpretations.

RESULTS

All study areas experienced a decline in low marsh from 1974 to 2004 and a gain in tidal flats, while all areas, except Cos Cob Harbor, also experienced a loss in high marsh (Table 1). Figures 2 through 7 show the changes in low marsh, high marsh, and tidal flat at various intervals over the past 30 years.

Canfield Island Cove was unique in that it had a small gain in open water (0.22 acres) and a gain in palustrine tidal wetland (0.31 acres). Over the 30-year study period, it experienced a 26% gain in tidal flat, while losing 27% of its low marsh and about 4% of its high marsh. Aquatic beds appeared to decline by nearly 40%. Aerial photos for 1974 and 2000 are provided in Appendix B to illustrate the changes in these wetlands.

Cos Cob Harbor was the only study estuary to show a gain in high marsh from 1974-2004, with a negligible 0.4-acre gain (2.5% increase). Tidal flat acreage increased by about 5 acres (30% gain), largely at the expense of low marsh which declined by 30%.

Five Mile River gained nearly 4 acres (67%) of tidal flat that formed in areas of former marsh. Nearly half of the low marsh was converted to tidal flat as was nearly one-fifth of its high marsh.

Similarly, Grays Creek estuary lost low marsh and high marsh to tidal flat which increased in acreage by 37%. Over half of the low marsh and about one-third of the high marsh acreage declined over the 30-year study period. Aerial photos for 1974 and 2000 are provided in Appendix B to illustrate the changes in these wetlands.

Greenwich Cove lost nearly 50% of its low marsh and only 8% of its high marsh from 1974-2004. These losses were countered by a nearly 11-acre gain (19%) in tidal flat.

Scott Cove, like the other areas in this study, experienced a gain in tidal flat at the expense of salt marsh. The nearly 17-acre gain in the former was the result of losses of 16 acres of low marsh and about 1 acre of high marsh. This was the largest acreage loss of low marsh among the six study areas.

Table 1. Acreage changes in study salt marshes from 1974 to 2004.

Salt Marsh System	Marsh Zone	Acreage							Overall Acreage Change (% Change)
		1974	1981	1986	1990	1995	2000	2004	
Canfield Island Cove	Tidal Flat	32.15	32.72	34.58	37.58	38.16	39.87	40.51	+8.36 (26.0)
	Low Marsh	27.61	27.08	25.36	22.53	21.90	20.62	20.06	-7.55 (27.3)
	High Marsh	48.13	47.71	47.25	47.07	46.71	46.36	46.42	-1.71 (3.5)
	Open Water	14.95	14.95	14.95	14.87	14.89	14.95	15.17	+0.22 (1.5)
	Aquatic Bed	0.80	0.75	0.78	0.78	0.78	0.81	0.49	-0.31 (38.8)
	Beaches	0.50	0.41	0.45	0.43	0.47	0.47	0.47	-0.03 (6.0)
	Palustrine Tidal	0.00	0.00	0.45	0.53	0.84	0.31	0.31	+0.31 (na)
Cos Cob Harbor	Tidal Flat	17.41	19.33	21.68	22.40	22.27	22.70	22.67	+5.26 (30.2)
	Beach	73.57	73.57	73.57	73.57	73.57	73.57	73.57	0.00 (0.0)
	Rocky Shore	0.24	0.24	0.24	0.24	0.24	0.24	0.24	0.00 (0.0)
	Low Marsh	19.38	17.09	14.77	13.88	13.90	13.56	13.58	-5.80 (29.9)
	High Marsh	15.85	16.15	15.94	16.19	16.30	16.25	16.25	+0.40 (2.5)
	Aquatic Bed	16.55	16.61	16.69	16.61	16.61	16.58	16.58	+0.03 (0.0)
Five Mile River	Tidal Flat	5.78	6.79	7.22	8.59	9.54	9.63	9.63	+3.85 (66.6)
	Low Marsh	5.75	5.38	5.33	4.23	2.97	2.93	3.04	-2.71 (47.1)
	High Marsh	6.56	5.92	5.53	5.27	5.53	5.48	5.37	-1.19 (18.1)
Grays Creek	Tidal Flat	18.36	20.15	21.48	23.31	24.17	24.95	25.21	+6.85 (37.3)
	Beach	0.41	0.37	0.31	0.32	0.35	0.35	0.32	-0.09 (22.0)
	Low Marsh	7.57	5.99	6.05	4.94	4.09	3.66	3.52	-4.05 (53.5)
	High Marsh	8.22	8.06	6.73	5.99	5.89	5.52	5.52	-2.70 (32.8)
	Aquatic Bed	0.07	0.07	0.07	0.07	0.13	0.15	0.07	0.00 (0.0)
	Open Water	0.58	0.58	0.58	0.58	0.58	0.58	0.58	0.00 (0.0)

Greenwich Cove							
Tidal Flat	56.39	58.95	62.84	64.35	66.11	67.50	67.12	+10.73 (19.0)
Beach	2.92	2.90	3.10	2.84	2.98	2.42	2.91	-0.01 (0.0)
Low Marsh	19.62	17.09	13.48	12.35	11.04	10.50	10.40	-9.22 (47.0)
High Marsh	21.30	21.01	20.52	20.40	19.81	19.52	19.52	-1.78 (8.4)
Open Water	14.79	14.79	14.79	14.79	14.79	14.79	14.79	0.00 (0.0)
Aquatic Bed	3.41	3.41	3.41	3.41	3.41	3.41	3.41	0.00 (0.0)
Scott Cove								
Tidal Flat	71.67	83.48	83.93	88.65	88.23	88.46	88.46	+16.79 (23.4)
Low Marsh	33.39	21.87	21.76	17.01	17.44	17.22	17.22	-16.17 (48.4)
High Marsh	16.39	16.09	15.75	15.79	15.72	15.72	15.72	-0.67 (4.1)
Open Water	3.03	3.03	3.03	3.03	3.03	3.03	3.03	0.00 (0.0)

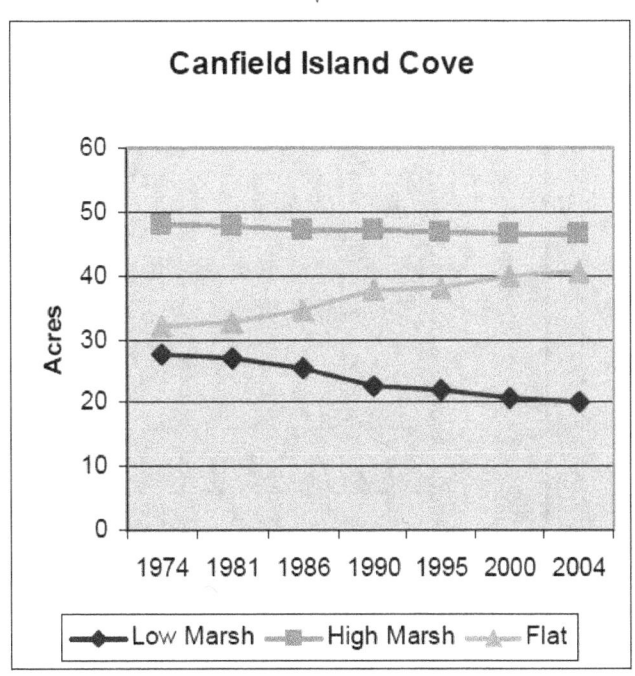

Figure 2. Trends for Canfield Island Cove.

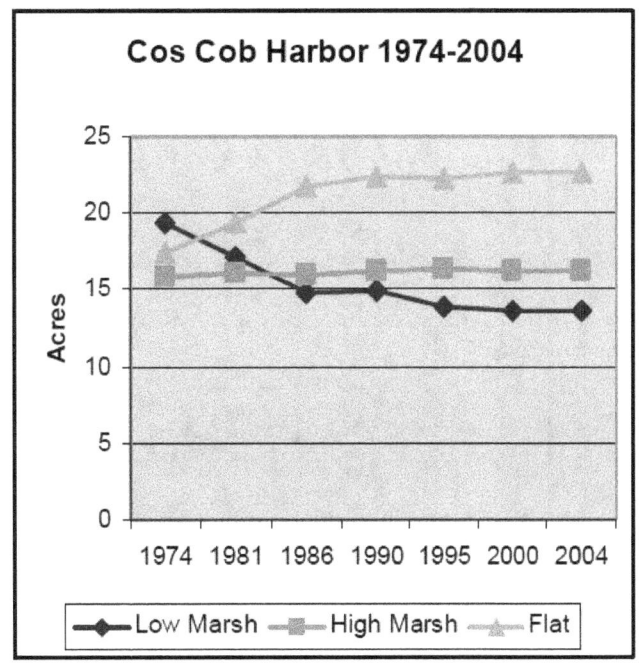

Figure 3. Trends for Cos Cob Harbor.

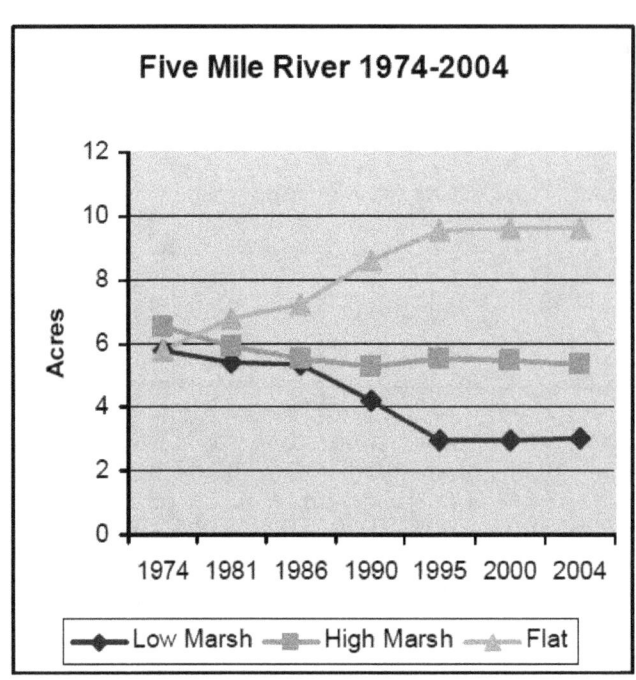

Figure 4. Trends for Five Mile River.

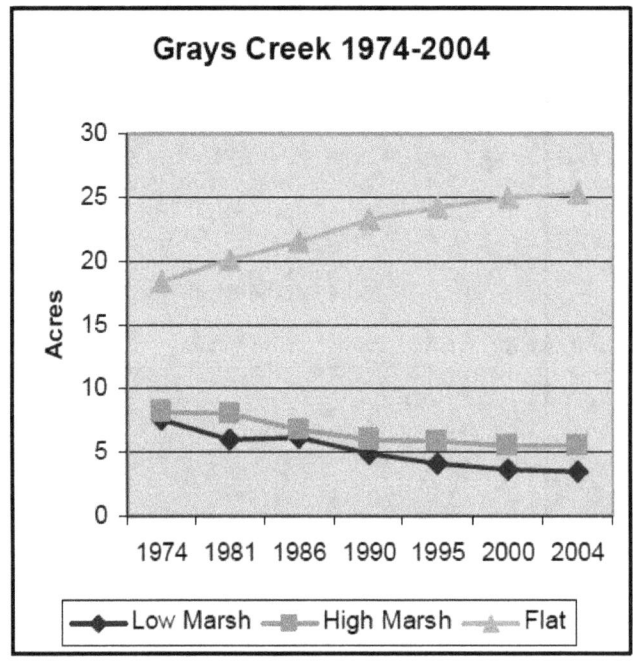

Figure 5. Trends for Grays Creek.

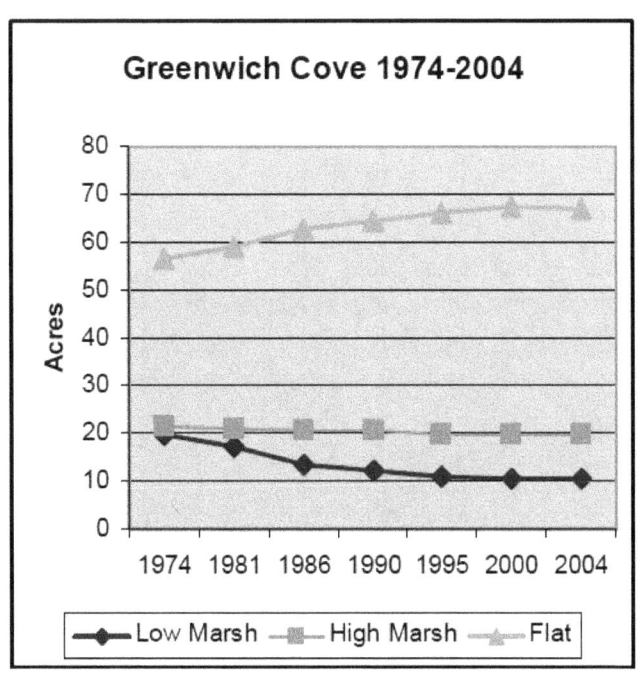

Figure 6. Trends for Greenwich Cove.

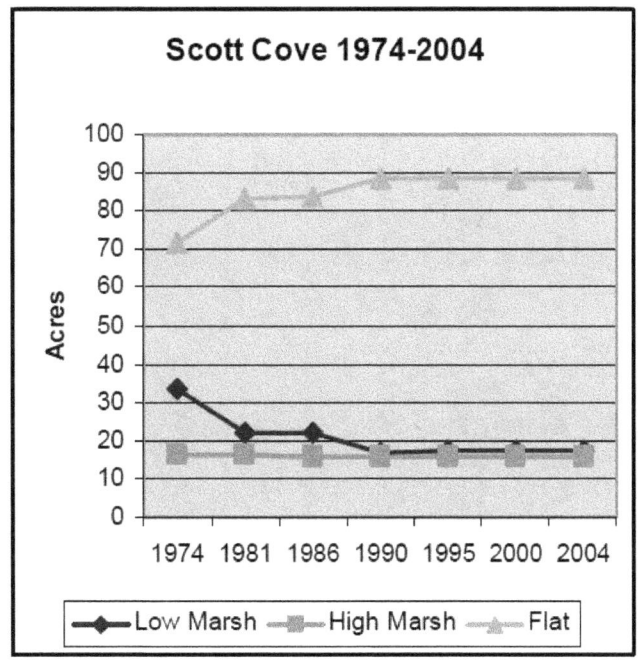

Figure 7. Trends for Scott Cove.

APPENDICES.

Appendix A. Maps showing location of study areas.

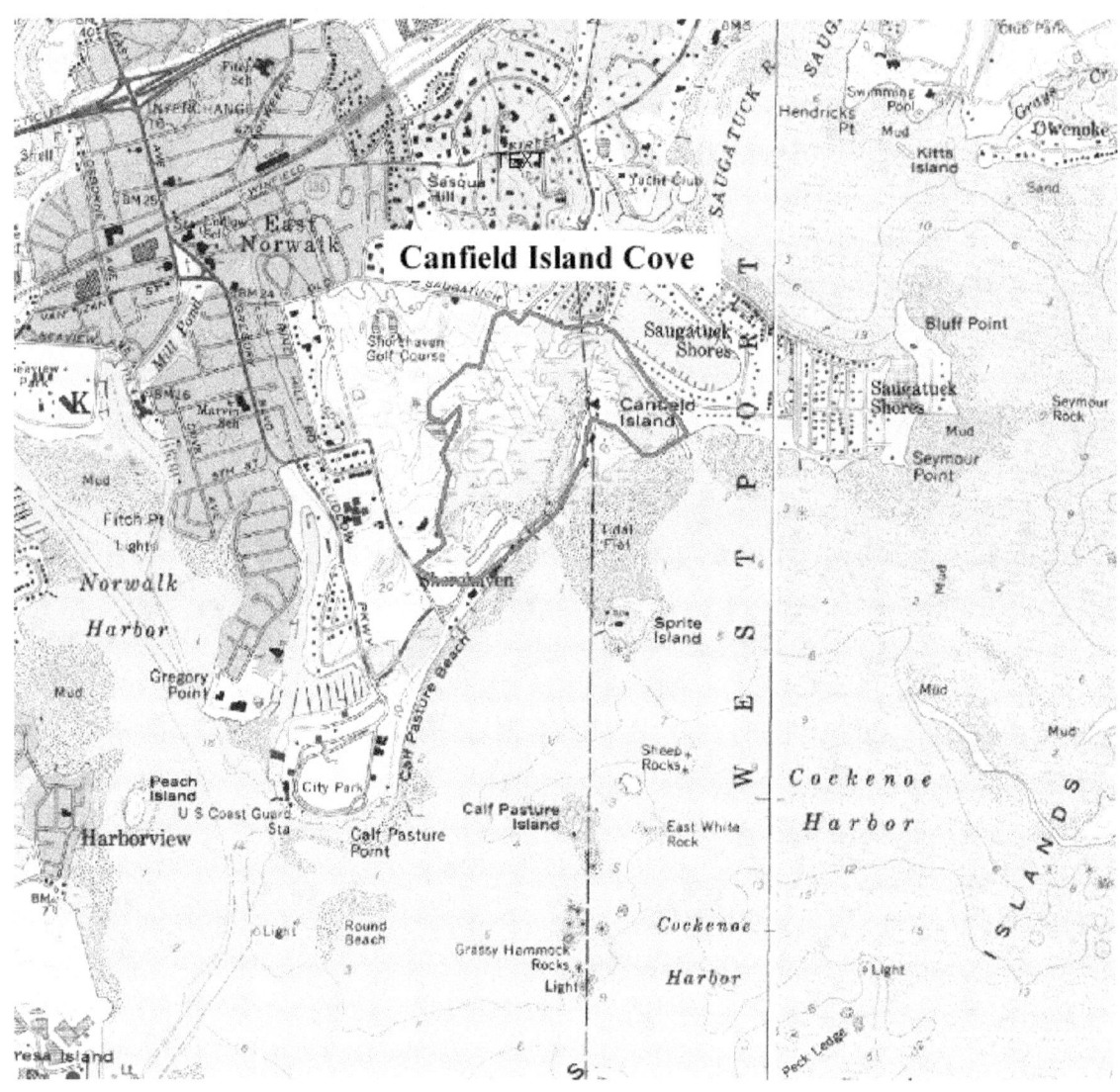

Canfield Island Cove

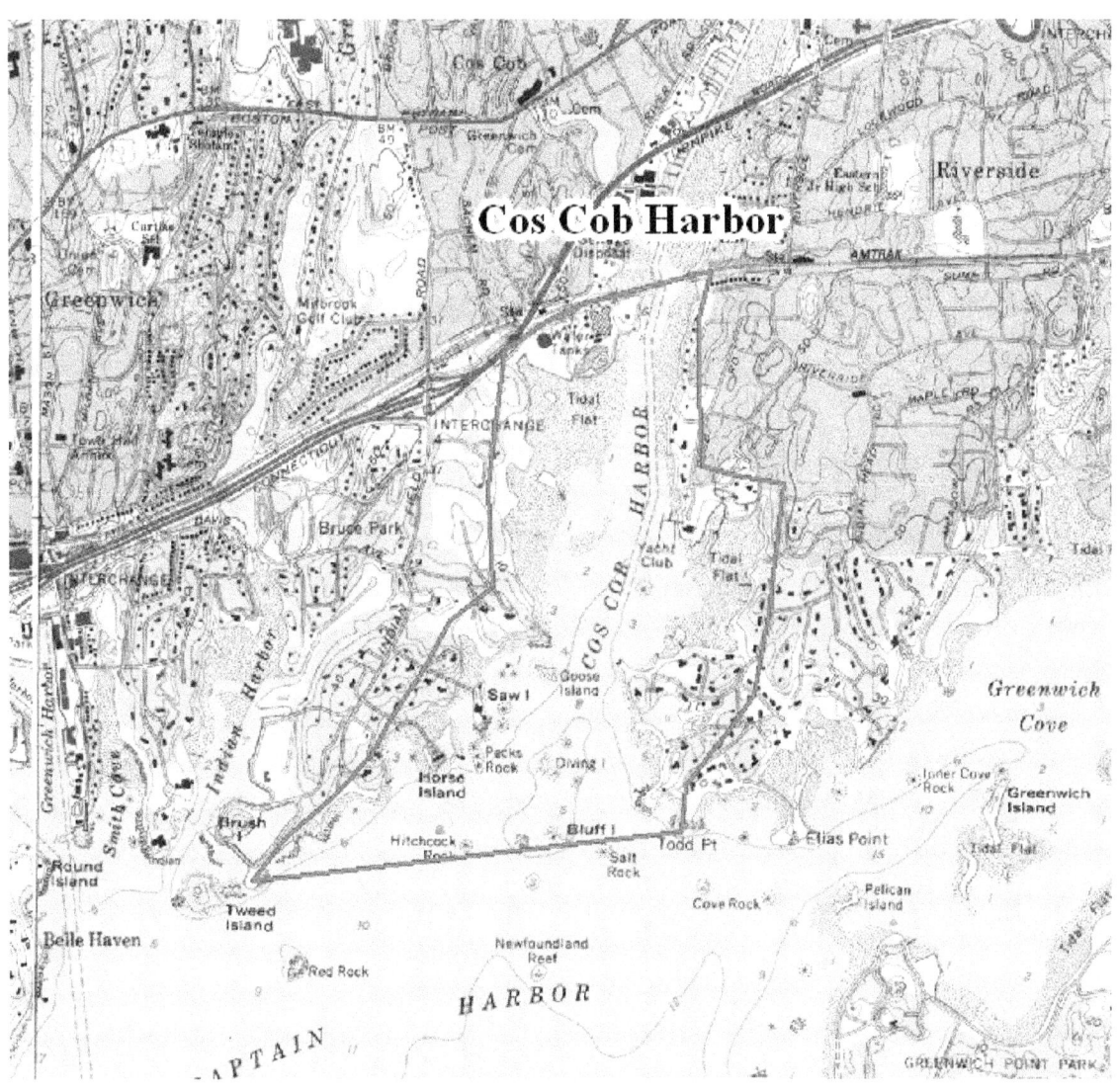

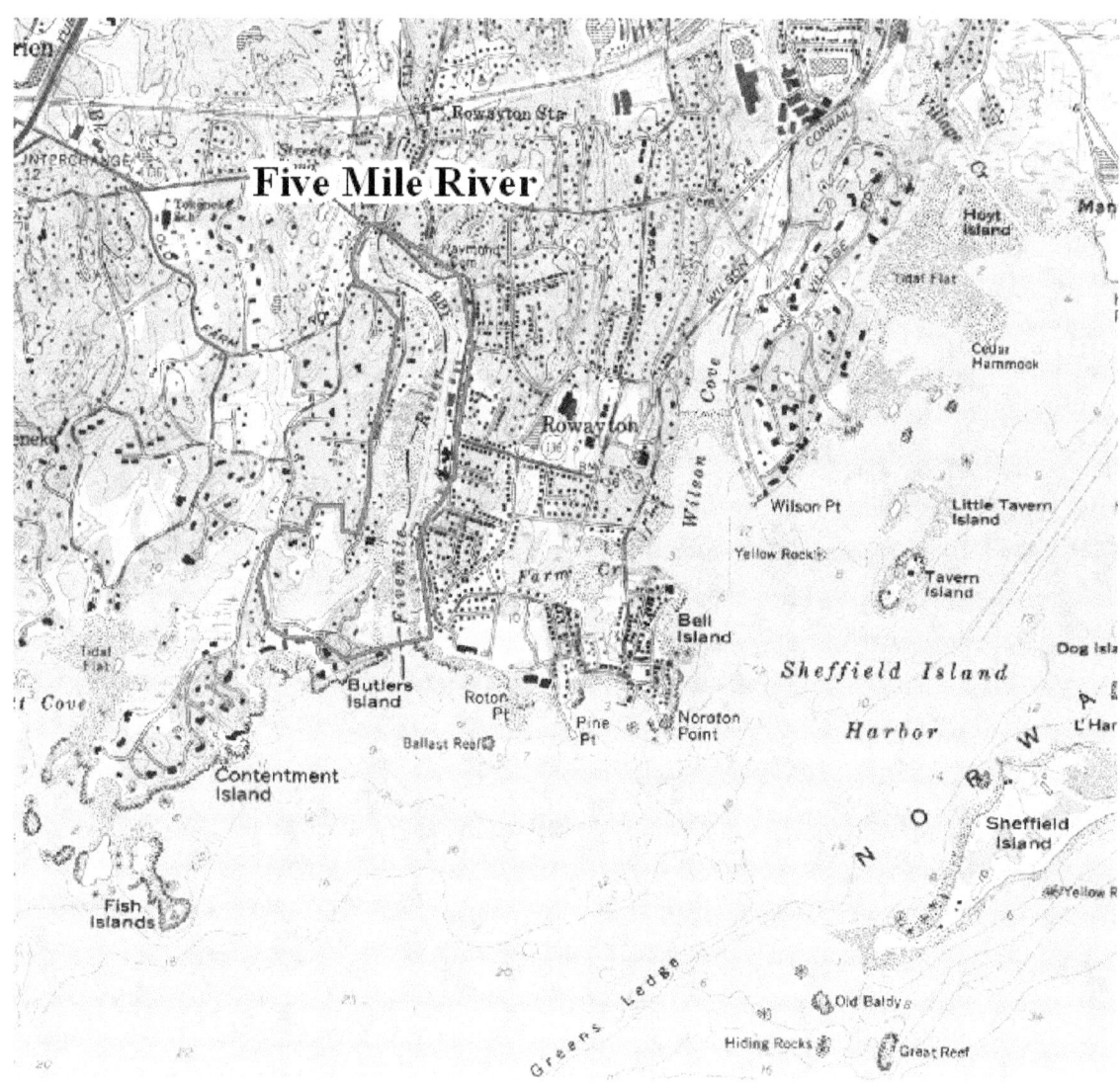

Five Mile River

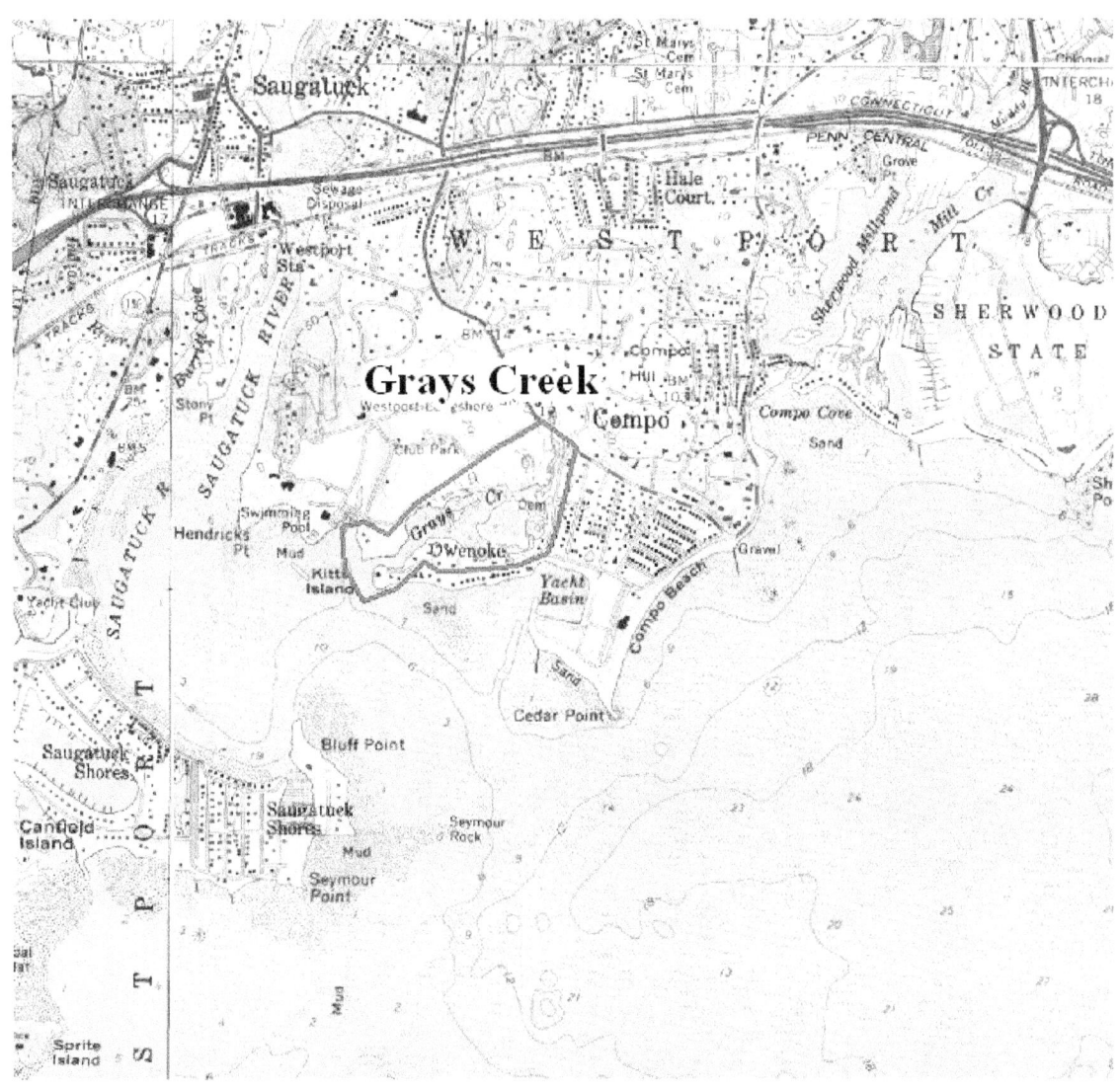

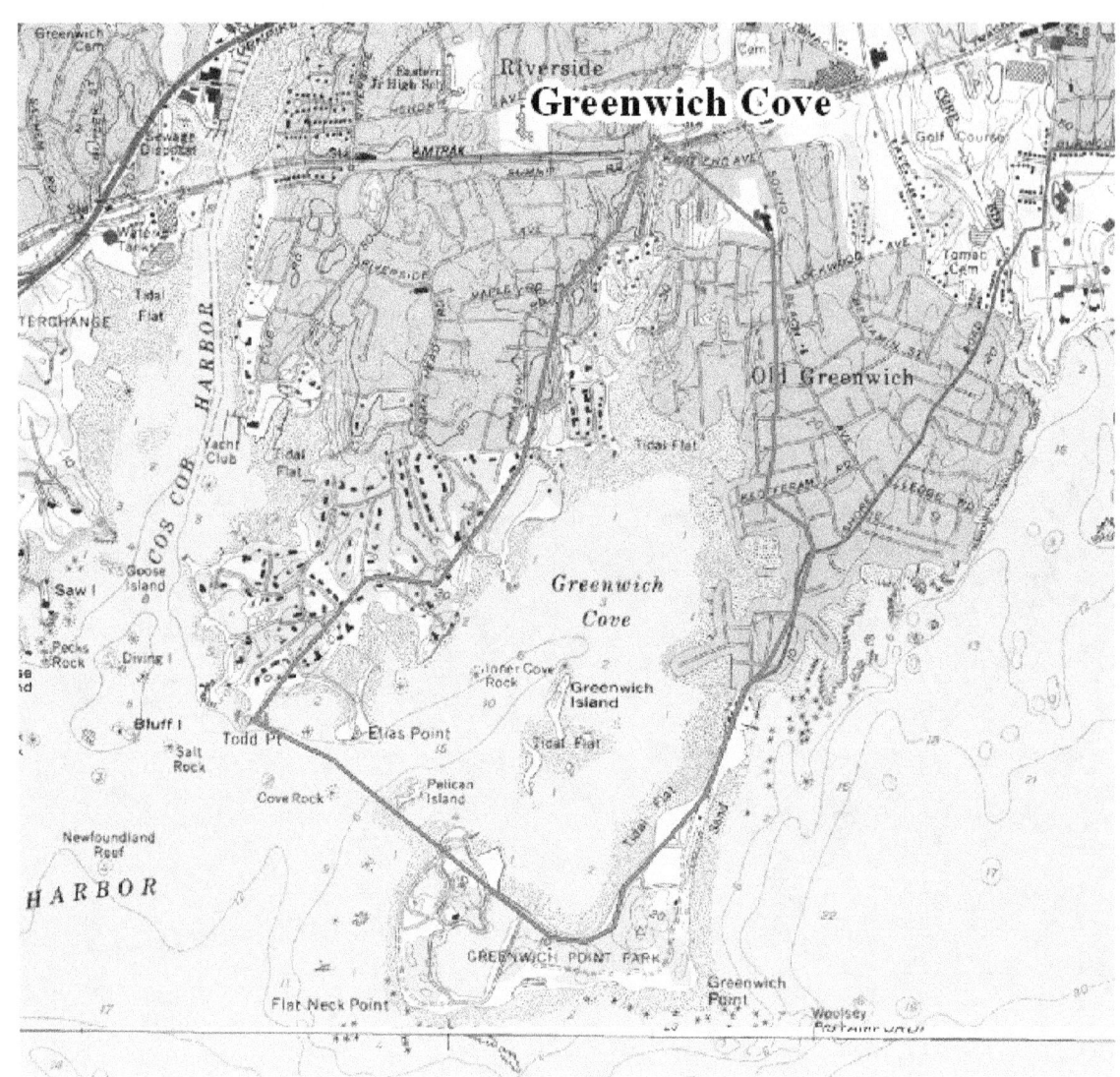

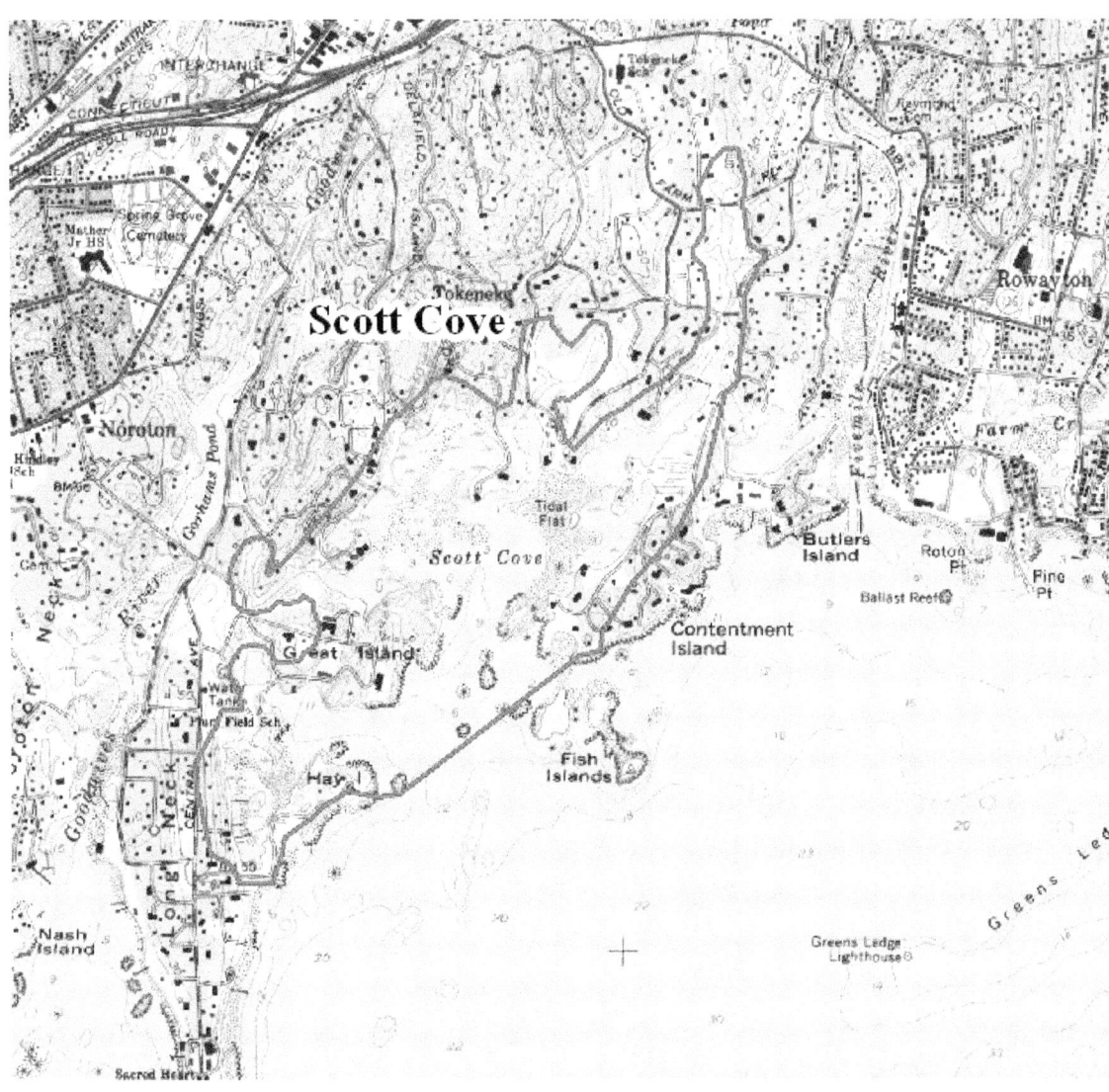

Appendix B. Aerial photos for Canfield Island Cove and Grays Creek (1974 vs. 2000).

CANFIELD ISLAND COVE – YR 1974 (ABOVE), YR 2000 (BELOW)

GRAYS CREEK - YR 1974 (ABOVE), YR 2000 (BELOW)

www.ingramcontent.com/pod-product-compliance
Lightning Source LLC
Chambersburg PA
CBHW081153290526
45795CB00008B/2908